Successful STUDENT RECRUITMENT *with* GOOGLE ADS

The Essential Guide

GUUS GOORTS

Successful student recruitment with Google Ads: The essential guide
By Guus Goorts
ISBN: 9789090328409

First edition –2020

Published by:
Adapt Business Innovatie BV
Broederplein 35a
3702 CD Zeist
The Netherlands
innovatie.adapt.nl

Find updates and additional resources related to the content of this book at guusgoorts.com.

Successful STUDENT RECRUITMENT *with* GOOGLE ADS

The Essential Guide

CONTENTS

Acknowledgements

My name is on the cover, but no book is the result of just one person's efforts. I'd particularly like to thank Vicky Lewis and Richard Conaway for their thorough reviews of earlier versions and thoughtful feedback. Furthermore, this book came into being through the direct and indirect support of my colleagues at Adapt Innovatie: Niels Huismans, Laurens van Piggelen and Rebecca Belderok. I've also drawn inspiration from my conversations with Hung Le, Josep Mas, my wife Yiran You and many others.

1

Introduction

1.1 WHY THIS BOOK?

In the past years I've supported education marketers tasked with student recruitment for a variety of education providers, such as universities, colleges and language schools.

While my expertise is in online marketing, I have seen first-hand that they need to juggle many balls. While dealing with agents, study fairs, social media, open days, webinars and printed brochures, they remain responsible for bringing the right number and the right type of new students to their institution, every year.

In this book I cover the essentials of Search Engine Advertising (SEA) and integrate them into an education marketer's framework. Whether you intend to set up a campaign on your own, work together with an online marketer or outsource a campaign to an external party, my goal is for you to know which questions to ask and what to pay attention to in order to make SEA contribute to the overall success of your student recruitment efforts.

Note: In this book, I sometimes use "university" as shorthand for "educational institution". As long as you're tasked with recruiting students, you'll find plenty of useful material in this book – whether you work at a university, college, technical institute or language school.

1.2 WHY FOCUS ON SEA?

There are three reasons why this book takes SEA campaigns as its focal point.

SEA can eat up a big chunk of the budget

The moment you decide to go with SEA, the budget spent on it can grow pretty rapidly.

For example, some larger Dutch universities spend €100–€200 thousand a year on SEA. Budget outlays of this size deserve attention to make sure they're put to good use.

Most SEA campaigns have lots of room for improvement

Many of the search advertising campaigns run by education providers are poorly managed. Keeping in mind the budget dedicated to them, this represents a serious waste. We have analysed the campaigns of universities in the Netherlands and Belgium, and found that **88% had at least one major flaw** in them, as detailed in the figure below.

Benchmarking SEA campaigns of 26 universities

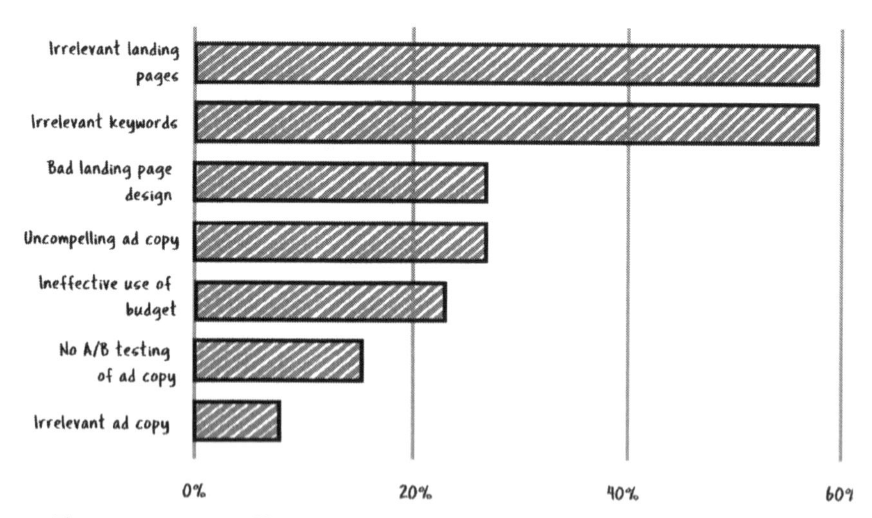

1.1 The most common problems encountered in the SEA campaigns of 26 Dutch and Belgian universities. The graph is based on our own investigation using publicly available data. Note that the graph only details operational issues. It doesn't examine whether, from a strategic point of view, SEA was the best investment for these institutes.

This brings us to the third reason for making SEA our focal point.

SEA campaigns need a strategy and well-defined processes

Successful SEA campaigns don't just happen. To be successful, they need to bring the **right people** to **great landing pages**, and schools have to **follow up consistently**.

There is a lot of literature on how to improve paid search campaigns in general. But, as far as I know, there is no book that specifically covers SEA for higher education providers and describes what needs to happen **before ads are written** or **after the ad click**.

In summary, while education providers invest significant budgets in search advertising, the return often amounts to only a fraction of what's possible. My goal for this book is to help you as an education marketer to realise the true potential of SEA.

1.3 WHAT TO EXPECT IN THIS BOOK

This book consists of two parts.

In Section 1, I'll cover the complete online recruitment process in broad strokes, focussing on how everything fits together. This section covers all marketing-related issues that are relevant for SEA. For example, to keep improving your SEA campaigns, you need to decide which Key Performance Indicators (KPIs) to track and how to measure them.

Section 2 goes into detail about SEA campaigns: how to plan, set up and optimise them; how to use campaigns for international recruitment; and how to collaborate successfully with a marketing agency.

You might think that the digital marketing landscape is changing so fast that it's completely different every year. However, the fundamentals are relatively stable: education providers need to package a compelling offer and get it in front of the right audience. This book focuses more on timeless principles than on the latest tips and tricks. To stay updated about current best practices, have a look at my author website **guusgoorts.com** and subscribe to receive updates.

SECTION I

OVERVIEW OF ONLINE STUDENT RECRUITMENT

2

Education marketing as a process

2.1 THE EDUCATION MARKETING PROCESS: AN OVERVIEW

The aim of the following model is to help you understand how all of the marketing tactics fit into the overall recruitment picture.

Process diagram of education marketing

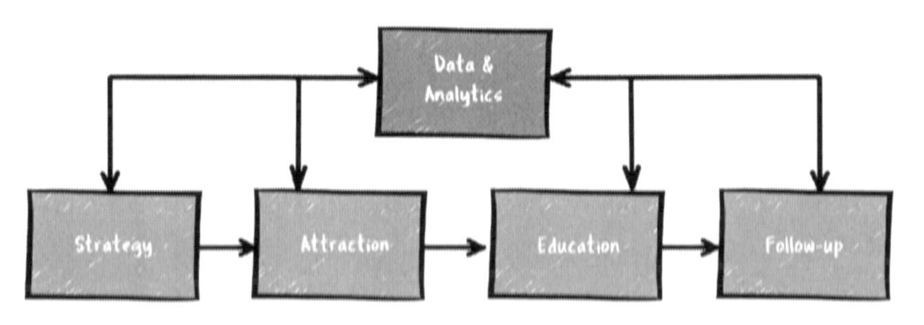

2.1 Model of the overall education marketing process.

Strategy

Before getting started, you need to set goals. You also have to know the strengths you can build on, your key areas of focus (which countries, specific groups of prospective students and programmes) and what you expect to achieve. When everyone involved can refer to a concise strategic brief, your recruitment effort will stay focused, even if there are many moving parts.

Analytics

How do you know you're on track to achieve your strategic goals? As part of your strategy, you need to define your goals in terms of KPIs. These could include

- website visits,
- open day visitors,
- webinar participants,
- completed applications,
- offers sent,
- offers accepted,
- new students enrolled.

Analytics is about defining how you're going to **keep track** of these KPIs and report them.

Attraction

With your strategy and measurement procedures in place, you now need to **get noticed by prospective students**. This can be done through countless channels, including offline and online advertising, search engine optimisation and media coverage. SEA falls into this segment.

Education

Just getting people's attention through your attraction efforts is not enough. If prospective students click on an ad, what will they find on the website? If they come to an event, what's their experience going to be like? The Education part of your process is about the **contents** of your marketing effort. You need to make sure all the essential topics are covered.

Follow-up

Choosing what to study and where is a high-stakes decision for prospective students. That's why they usually need more than a single interaction before they make their final decision.

Follow-up is about **what happens after the first website visit**. Do you have a plan for engaging with prospective students on an ongoing basis? This could be through retargeting, email updates or messenger marketing, to name a few options.

2.2 CONCLUSION

SEA belongs to the **attraction** stage of a larger marketing process. In the end your results are going to be only as strong as the weakest link in the chain: strategy, analytics, attraction, education and follow-up. If there are gaps in the process, you'll end up pouring water into a leaky bucket – no matter how great your search campaign is.

2.2 Your student recruitment process is only as strong as its weakest link

3

Strategy

If sea is the car, strategy is the navigation system. To reach your final destination, you need to decide where you want to go (objectives) and which route to take to get there (strategic choices).

It's natural to get obsessed with the car while not paying enough attention to the route to be taken. The Lamborghini captures our imagination, but what use is it if you end up in a traffic jam or at a dead end? Strategy is mapping out the journey ahead and switching to your bicycle if it happens to be the fastest option.

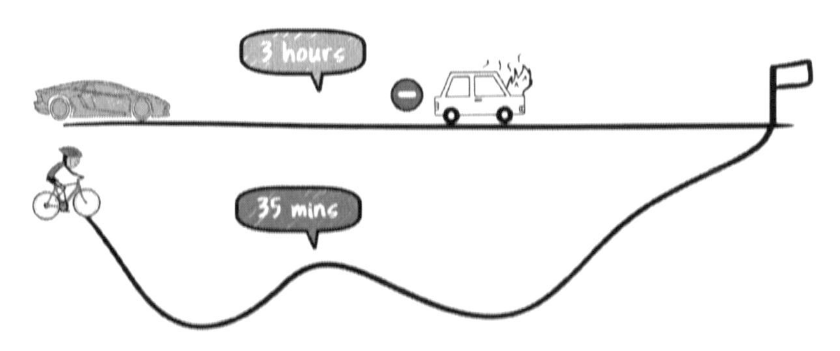

3.1 Strategy: Establish a goal and determine the most efficient way of getting there.

Before any communication goes out, you need to be clear about your objectives and what you have to offer. With a clearly defined strategy, you know who to reach out to and what to say to them.

3.1 KEY STRATEGIC QUESTIONS

The word "strategy" can mean different things to different people. But let's not overcomplicate things: just make sure you agree internally on the questions below. By **documenting** the answers to these questions for each programme, you will have a **brief** that can be shared with everyone who is involved in the recruitment effort, from internal staff to external contractors.

Who are our ideal students?

Which types of student are most likely to complete the programme successfully? Write up a short profile of each of your ideal student types that you want to reach out to.

The following questions can help you make up a meaningful description:

- If you look at the current top 20% of the graduates from the programme, what do they have in common?
- Are there groups of students or demographics that you want to focus on?
- How did these students find out about your institution and programme?
- What made them choose to pursue this programme at this institution?

You may find answers by

- interrogating your institution's CRM systems;
- consulting external data sources to uncover enrolment trends;
- looking at your current top students to see what they have in common;

Who are our competitors?

These could be institutions

- in the same area that offer the same or similar programmes,
- elsewhere that offer similar programmes,nearby or elsewhere that provide online programmes, internships or on-the-job training programmes.

What are our unique selling points?

After you've answered the previous two questions, you'll have a good understanding of who your ideal students are; what they value; and the choices before them, beyond the courses you offer. Knowing all of this, you need to ask the following: What advantages do you have to offer? Could you further develop your programmes to distinguish yourself from the other available options?

Document the top two or three reasons why prospective students should pick your institution. By making the key selling points explicit, you make it possible for everyone involved in recruiting students for a particular programme to make use of them. This holds for both team members and external suppliers. And it also holds for all types of contexts, including search advertising campaigns, your website and the press. This is key to getting the most out of any media exposure you receive.

How many students do we want to recruit for this programme one, two and five years from now?

No matter how much action you take today, it takes time for results to materialise. If you plant a hundred fruit trees today; none will bear fruit next year. Each of the trees will take 3-5 years to start bearing fruit. Similarly, some of the most impactful actions you can take to raise student numbers can take three to five years to show results. For example, the HAN University of Applied Sciences sends a technology bus to visit secondary schools in its surrounding region. By engaging with prospective students several years before graduation, they hope to influence these students' choices of subject and spark an interest in studying technology at HAN after their graduation.

In the short run, you can achieve quick results by making yourself more visible and clearly spelling out the benefits of your programmes. But ultimately, you'll be talking to those prospective students who are already interested in the subject matter of your programme and are open to studying at your institution, in your area. This limits the potential.

On a time scale of several years, you can enlarge the number of prospective students by sparking initial interest in your programmes and institution. Inspire students who are still a few years away from graduating from secondary school and they may choose different prerequisite courses. In this way you'll increase your institution's long-term potential. This is why it's important to have a plan with actions aimed at both short-term and long-term improvement.

What budget do we have available to make this happen?

If you know the results you're aiming for in the short, intermediate and long term, you can work backwards to define the actions you need to take to achieve them. A well-defined strategy can help achieve a lot more with the budget available because it aligns your actions with your goals and helps you make clear choices. But it's important to request and get the budget you require. If your institution has the goal of doubling student numbers in five years but no budget for additional actions, it's not really a goal.

It's fairly straightforward to estimate the budget required. In Chapter 9, I'll share how to budget for search advertising campaigns.

What are our KPIs?

While long-term goals are important for overall direction, how do you know you're on course to achieve them?

When you enter a destination and mode of transport into Google Maps, it gives you a projected arrival time. During your journey there, the software keeps track of your location and traffic conditions, and adjusts the projected arrival time based on how far you have progressed at a given time. Similarly, your long-term goals need to be broken down into shorter-term measures so that you can check to make sure you're on track. You should choose three to five measures. Set goals for them at given intervals, and keep track of how things are proceeding. Here are a number of possible KPIs:

- website visits,
- open day visitors,
- webinar participants,

- offers sent,
- new students enrolled.

3.2 CONCLUSION

Wherever you may want to go, you won't arrive without a documented strategy. Once you have written down the answers to the questions listed above, they will help create impact for everything you do.

The strategy document should be shared widely within your team and with external contractors such as agencies. It will become an important point of reference and a measuring stick for every event, web page or campaign.

4

Data and analytics

Having goals and objectives is great, but let's face it: things often work out differently in the real world. Measure performance and you'll be able to see what works and what doesn't – and to double down on what works. Tracking performance helps to keep you on track to achieving your objectives. But what you measure will make a big difference.

To give you two hypothetical examples, analytics may tell you that

- students from Bulgaria are highly likely to successfully complete your bachelor of automotive engineering, and
- none of the leads that came in through your Instagram campaign actually applied for a programme.

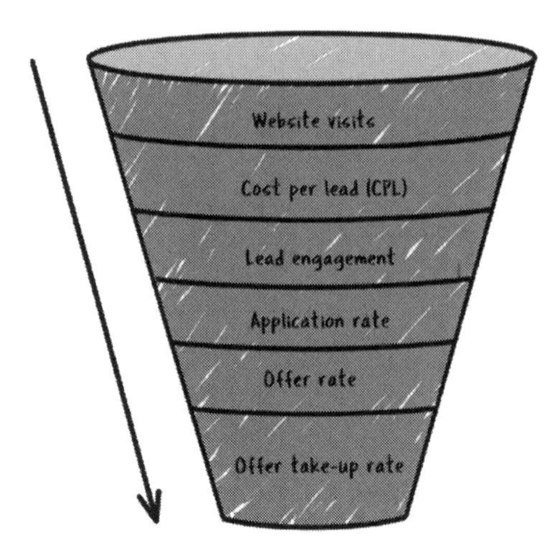

4.1 KPIs to keep track of as prospective students progress towards enrolment.

The metrics you keep track of don't only determine what you know: they also dictate what you and your team will prioritise. The key metrics to keep track of in the context of Google search ads are:

1. cost per lead (CPL),
2. lead engagement,
3. application rate,
4. offers rate,
5. offer take-up rate.

As you see, they follow the marketing funnel (figure 4.1) from initial exposure to offers taken up. I'll now go on to cover each of them in more detail below.

4.1 COST PER LEAD (CPL)

What is it?

How much does it cost to generate one enquiry or brochure download? How does the cost differ between

- channels (e.g. your SEA campaign vs. Facebook ads), and
- target groups (e.g. national students vs. students from Bulgaria)?

Why is it important?

CPL is a good metric for **assessing the effectiveness of a campaign**. It compares the "output" of a campaign to what it costs. There are high- and low-quality leads, but **leads are much more meaningful than clicks**. Those who make an enquiry (i.e. who become leads) have visited your website, read some content and taken action to further the relationship.

CPL is also an **important building block for establishing your advertising budget**. If you know (1) how many leads it takes to get an enrolment and (2) how much it costs to acquire one additional lead, then you can derive the budget required to reach your goal.

How do you calculate CPL?

Do this as follows:

CPL = (total campaign cost) ÷ (number of leads acquired)

Number of leads acquired. How many downloads, brochure requests, subscribers and/or enquiries did the campaign bring in? If all the traffic for a given campaign goes to a unique landing page or form, you can simply count the number of leads. If the campaign shares a form with other types of traffic, you'll need to make sure that whenever a submission is made, the source is registered. I'll go into more detail about how to do this in Part II, Section 10.

Total cost of campaign. What do you spend to run the campaign? This figure should include

- the advertising costs paid to Google, Facebook or other platforms; and
- the cost of producing the creatives, and the costs for copywriting and campaign management.

Automate it.

When set up correctly, Google Ads can calculate CPL automatically and even give you the figures for specific keywords, landing pages and ad copies. I'll say more about how to do this in Chapter 9.

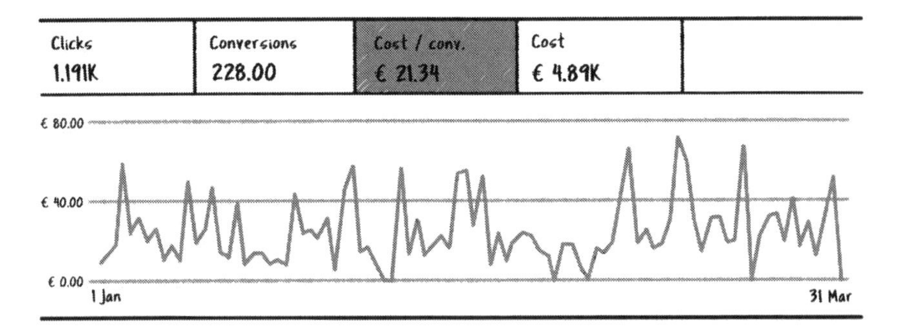

4.2 With some basic set-up, Google will calculate metrics such as cost per conversion for you.

Terminology issues.

What does the word "lead" mean in your organisation? Does it refer to someone who subscribes to email updates? Or do you use the term to refer to prospective students who show up on your open day? Either is fine, but don't throw both numbers on the same stack as this would make the CPL figures meaningless. To avoid confusion, it's better to ditch the term "lead" and refer to the specific item involved, for example "cost per open day visitor" or "cost per enquiry".

4.2 LEAD ENGAGEMENT

What is it?

Lead engagement is a measure of how active leads are after they are acquired. Individual organisations may define the term somewhat differently, but the metric will show up as a percentage of the total number of leads who took action after enquiring, for example, by attending an open day.

Why is it important?

When a lead engages further with you, he or she hits another milestone on the path to becoming one of your students. While it's great to have lots of people on your mailing list, you want as many of them as possible to take the next step.

If lead engagement is low, it may mean you didn't acquire the right kinds of leads to start with or that you haven't paid enough attention to following up with them.

While every situation is different, I'd pay serious attention if lead engagement falls below 30%.

How do you calculate lead engagement?

It can be calculated as follows:

Lead engagement = (leads that took a specified action) ÷ (total number of leads)

If you have a CRM set up, it may report the figure automatically on a dashboard. But you can also calculate it manually, once or a few times a year. To do this, count the total number of consequent actions (e.g. RSVPs for open days) in a period and divide this number by the number of leads acquired in that same period.

4.3 APPLICATION RATE

What is it?

The percentage of leads that submit a valid application.

Why is it important?

Applying is the natural next step on the path to becoming a student. You will want to know if a good percentage of the people who enquired and were in touch with you actually ended up applying for the course. If this figure is low, it may point to a problem in the preceding steps. The sooner you find out there is a problem, the sooner you can fix it. It's that simple.

How do you calculate it?

Application rate is calculated by dividing the yearly number of applications by the number of leads:

Application rate = (number of applications) ÷ (number of leads)

Again, depending on your set-up, this number can be calculated either automatically or manually.

4.4 OFFER RATE

What is it?

The offer rate is the percentage of applications that are accepted.

Why is it important?

Especially if your institution is competitive to get into, this number can give you a good idea of the quality of applicants that the different campaigns manage to attract.

If certain campaigns bring in lots of applications but very few of these applications get accepted, it may mean that the campaign was aimed at the wrong demographic or that expectations were unrealistic.

How do you calculate it?

The number of offers given can be calculated as follows:

Offer rate = (offers given) ÷ (applications received)

4.5 OFFER TAKE-UP RATE

What is it?

The percentage of the total number of offers given out that are actually accepted.

Why is it important?

Just because you extend an offer doesn't mean that you've got yourself a new student. Prospective students may apply to multiple institutions. If there is a large gap between offers extended and students starting the programme, you may need to do a better job of staying in touch with offer holders and getting them started. Also, this gap may point to something that puts you at a disadvantage compared to competing institutions. Perhaps they offer better facilities or more prestige. It can also have to do with how your offer was communicated and whether the offer holder was reassured in the period between offer and decision.

How do you calculate it?

You can calculate the offer take-up rate as follows:

Offer take-up rate = (offers accepted) ÷ (offers given)

4.6 CONCLUSION

Recruiting students for a programme is a process. To know whether the process is working well and to identify possible bottlenecks, you need to keep an eye on a number of KPIs along the way:

1. CPL,
2. lead engagement,
3. application rate,
4. offers given,
5. offer take-up rate.

5

Attraction

So far we've covered how to strategise and how to measure progress. Now it's time to make yourself known to the world. In the attraction stage the objective is to expose prospective students to your courses for the first time and to whet their appetite to find out more. This can be done in a hundred different ways, of which SEA is one.

1. search
2. early outreach
3. broad outreach

Each category of attraction methods has specific strengths. Search is laser-focused on the prospective students who are looking for your programme, right now. Early outreach and broad outreach cover a much broader group of potential students.

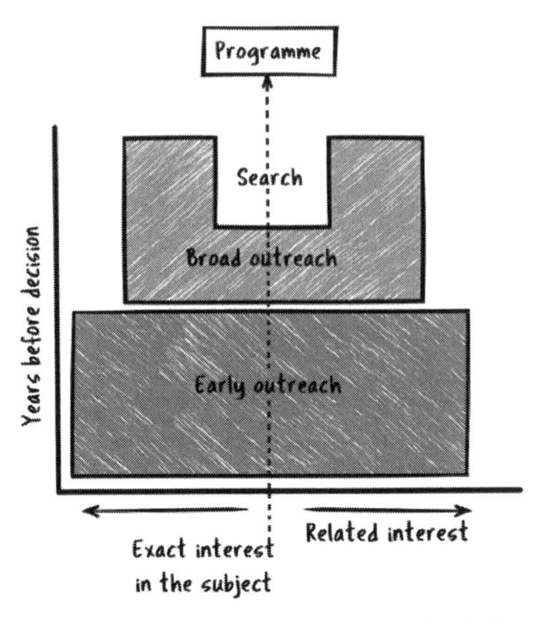

5.1 Campaign types, relative to the number of people they reach and how close these prospective students are to signing up for the programme you're advertising.

5.1 SEARCH

SEA falls under the "search" category, which also includes organic search and course comparison sites such as Studyportals and Hotcourses. People actively searching and comparing are most likely to become students. Someone who searches for "chemistry degree" is very likely to eventually enrol in a chemistry course and end up being a motivated student, be it at your institution or elsewhere. If you're insufficiently visible in searches, the effect on enrolment numbers is almost immediate.

On the flip side, search only covers a **small subset of people**. What about those who haven't decided yet what they're interested in? And what of those who have never thought of your institution? Search-based marketing methods are fairly useless for reaching them.

With search marketing, you can influence what shows up when a prospective student keys in a specific keyword. But you cannot influence what a given prospective student chooses to search for.

This is where early and broad outreach come in.

5.2 EARLY OUTREACH

Career choice isn't a matter of a single event. Prospective students' interests get shaped over many years before they finally decide where to apply. With early outreach institutions can get the ball rolling several years before students graduate from secondary school. Here are some examples:

- inviting students in their final year to be a "student for a day",
- giving talks at secondary schools,
- maintaining relationships with career advisers at secondary schools.

If I go back to my own choice of studies, I was greatly influenced by a 30-minute career talk by an entrepreneur. His stories, passion and imagination made me want to study business. When a neighbour found out I was visiting open days for business programmes, he arranged for me to be able to sit in on a problem-based learning session at Maastricht University. The rest is history.

Early outreach is an essential long-term attraction strategy. It can increase not only the number of applicants but also the quality and fit of the candidates. Reach them early enough, and you can still influence their choices of subjects in secondary school. But bear in mind that extra efforts in early outreach will only pay off after three to five years.

5.3 BROAD OUTREACH

For earlier results beyond what can be achieved with search alone, there is broad outreach. When prospective students are in the market for a certain type of degree, they might not have thought of your institution or the specific courses you offer. Many students aren't sure about what programme to pursue in the first place.

Here are some of the ways in which you're probably already conducting broad outreach:

- outdoor advertising,
- print ads,
- social media campaigns,
- online banner campaigns,
- radio ads.

The idea behind broad outreach is to cast a wide net and to "nudge" prospective students to consider a degree or institution they hadn't thought of yet. As a next step, they might visit your website or search for your institution's name.

5.4 CONCLUSION

Once you have a strategy and have defined your goals and how to measure them, it's time to go out and make sure prospective students know you exist. Attraction is all about being known by prospective students who are probably interested in the courses at your institution. Every year there are a limited number of prospective students "in the market". To gain maximum traction, you need to carry out the following:

1. **Search** – to be sure none of the prospective students most likely to enrol miss out on you;
2. **Early outreach** – to shape the interest of prospective students early on;
3. **Broad outreach** – to ignite the interest of those initially looking for different, though related programmes.

6

Education

After the attraction phase comes education. The prospective student who enters this phase already knows you exist and now sets out to learn more about you.

For education providers, the objective of this phase is to help prospective students decide whether any programme at your institution is right for them. It's a matter of putting the right student in the right place. This can also include discouraging some people from applying. If a student loves your institution for its history and the content of the courses you offer and decides to apply, that's a win. If another prospective student finds out that a programme elsewhere is a better fit for them, that's just as much a win.

What do students need to know to make a good decision? It's not just about answering every conceivable question: good presentation is just as important to "getting through" to each prospective student. I'll now go on to discuss

1. key subject areas to cover, and
2. presentation formats and timing.

6.1 KEY SUBJECT AREAS TO COVER

A common pitfall in the education stage is to be too narrowly focused on the academic aspects of what an institution has to offer. When people choose a college or university, they're also choosing an institution with its own culture, a new city and a new phase in their life. The more complete the picture you paint, the more confident prospective students will be about their decision. The key subject areas are

1. course information,
2. student and alumni stories,
3. information on life in the city and at the university,
4. practical information, and
5. information for parents.

I'll now go on to discuss cover each of these in more detail.

Course information

Each programme needs its own page that describes in broad terms

- what it is about,
- which topics will be covered,
- whom it is for, and
- what the admission criteria are.

Besides having pages for each programme, help prospective students find out which programmes are likely suited for them. A robust way to search, select and filter the programmes you offer to prospective students is a must. Especially if you have many courses to offer, find inspiration from travel and e-commerce websites and use faceted search. This allows people to narrow down the options by selecting a specific programme type, study mode, subject and course location.

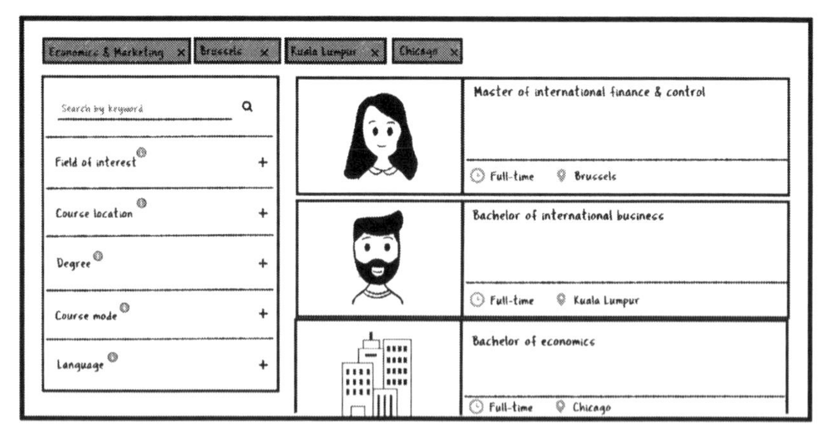

6.1 An example of how e-commerce style navigation can assist prospective students in finding the suitable programme.

You could go even deeper than this and offer an **online personal assessment quiz**. By asking a number of questions about a person's prior education, interests and career ambitions, you can help prospective students find out which courses would be a good fit for them.

Stories from current students and alumni

Course information tends to be dry: facts and more facts. And of course, the key facts need to be readily accessible. But it's hard for the human mind to process facts alone. You can make the same information easier to digest by interviewing students and alumni. The story format and emotional appeal will make readers remember the facts much better.

An interview can look at the issues from many angles:

- What does a day in your life as a student look like?
- Why did you choose to study at this institution?
- What are your ambitions?

People respond best to stories from people they can identify with, so make sure to include a variety of demographically diverse student profiles.

Life in the city and at university

For many students, starting on a degree marks the transition from living with their parents to living on their own. This can be scary, even overwhelming. You can help prospective students manage this anxiety by sharing information on what it's like to live in the area. This shouldn't be merely a sales pitch about what's so fantastic about the area but should include information on day-to-day life. Where do people hang out in their free time? What are some of the prominent buildings? What types of food is the region known for? The further afield prospective students come from, the harder it is for them to imagine what it's going to be like living and studying at your institution.

Practical information

The education phase of the recruitment process isn't only about creating a desire. Just because someone loves the idea of enrolling in a degree programme you offer doesn't mean they'll do it. Help prospective students overcome practical barriers by sharing how-to information, including how to apply for

- the programme,
- any available scholarships,
- housing, and
- health insurance.

Universities often link to external resources too soon and leave prospective students to figure things out on their own. By summarising the relevant information (e.g. how much do students generally pay for housing?), you can help lower the perceived practical barriers.

Information for parents

Around the world parents have a say in their children's choice of post-secondary education. In some cultures they even tend to be the main decision-maker. So be sure to address their "adult" questions, which tend to centre more around safety, career prospects and financing. You can make parents more comfortable by featuring interviews with parents of current students.

Many universities have a bilingual website, with information provided in the language of their country plus English. You might think this makes sense. After all, whoever applies should understand English well enough to be qualified for an English-language programme in the first place. But parents may not read English or not read it well. So if you are seriously planning to recruit in a given country, make sure to add at least a few pages with key content in that country's language.

6.2 PRESENTATION FORMATS

Recently, I ended up in a traffic jam and started to feel hungry. I was delighted to find that my wife had stacked some cookies in the compartment below the arm rest. Now, when I go to a restaurant, I expect a full meal. Of course, the latter is far more nutritious than a stack of cookies, but you're not always in a position to consume a full meal. The same holds for the way you present information to prospective students. Sometimes they are only able to digest bite-size pieces of information. At other times they've dedicated more time to learn about what you have to offer, and you can present them with formats that offer more depth.

Of course, you can produce almost limitless amounts of content. There are many presentation formats:

- web pages,
- video,
- social media posts,
- chatbots,
- brochures,
- events,
- webinars.

Here are some tips on how you can use them effectively.

Web pages

No matter what other content you publish, web pages are the foundation. The key general information about your institution, available programs, events and how to learn more should always be available in the form of web pages. All information should be in text form so that search engines can easily figure out what each page is about. In addition, you can embed videos and photos.

I recommend not going into too much detail on the web pages. You should certainly avoid publishing the entire course syllabus on the website. There are two reasons for this:

- **To avoid information overload**. More is less. If you prioritise the most important points, this information will get more attention and prospective students will be able to form a better picture.

- **To encourage deeper engagement**. There will be a moment when prospective students want to know more than what they've learned from the general information on the website. This signals serious interest. If more detailed information is only available upon request, prospective students who are seriously interested have a better reason to make themselves known to you by requesting a brochure or attending an event.

Video

People process information visually. Video is a great way to make your institution and the people in it seem real to prospective students. Unfortunately, videos are also time consuming to produce. So the message is "plan and repurpose". For example, you can convert the key content of your website into presentations and have someone present them on-screen. One day of recording can yield many videos. And if you include video stories, you can also convert them into blog posts and social media postings.

Social media posts

Social media posts can play a role in different phases: attraction, education and follow-up. They can consist of a mix of repurposed website content and videos, curated content from other sources and updates on events. Social media posts work best when there is a plan behind the content mix and the frequency of posting.

Chatbots

If you've ever tried to add a chat button on your institution's website, you'll probably have realised that answering each query is at most a good way to identify gaps in your content and to get to know your website visitors personally. But attending to every question personally is usually not feasible. Enter chatbots. It's still early days, but chatbots have great potential for helping prospective students navigate large, complex websites. For example, by asking a few closed questions, they can help prospective students identify where to go.

Brochures

Brochures can be the physical version of a programme page. It's easy to hand them out at student fairs and other events. If you offer a brochure download on your website, make sure the brochure actually contains something that can't be found on the programme page.

Events and webinars

At events prospective students can talk to current students and professors. This is a great way to build confidence and give them a sense of what studying at your institution is about.

If your aim is to recruit students further afield, webinars and virtual open days help to overcome the barrier of having to fly over for an open day.

6.3 CONCLUSION

If you're successful in the attraction stage, you'll be known to lots of prospective students who may be interested in entering a programme at your institution. The education stage is about making sure prospective students get the right information, at the right moment and in the right format, so that they'll be able to make the right decision about where to study. Those students who are particularly interested will contact you or attend events.

The next step in the recruitment process is to stay in touch with prospective students during the time they explore different options. I cover this in the next chapter: Follow-up.

7

Follow-up

IT HARDLY EVER HAPPENS that a prospective student visits a university website once and then immediately decides to apply. Choosing where to apply is a process, not an event.

It's crucial to keep your institution in prospective students' minds during this decision-making time, and that's where follow-up comes in. Unfortunately, follow-up is a part of the recruitment process where things often fall apart. In this chapter I will cover first the challenges that stand in the way of following up effectively and then the different ways in which you can stay in touch with prospective students during their decision-making journey.

7.1 CHALLENGES WITH FOLLOW-UP

The key obstacles to timely follow-up are

- lack of time,
- inadequate capture of contact details, and
- uncertainty about privacy laws, such as the General Data Protection Regulation (GDPR).

Lack of time

Does your team have enough time to answer all incoming enquiries within one business day? Timely follow-up is essential because it builds trust and supports prospective students in their decision-making process. If you answer late, the answer will probably have lost some of its relevance.

You can save time in these ways:

Display contact forms instead of email addresses

This streamlines the flow of questions immensely. Even the simplest contact forms can generate an email. And you can insert a few required fields and make sure you have the basic data needed to respond. Forms, unlike e-mails, can be tracked. This means you know how many enquiries are submitted, and you can verify whether they are answered in a timely way.

It's much better, of course, if web forms flow directly into a CRM system. This system can filter and categorise questions, and present staff with answer templates that already contain the answers for the most frequently asked questions, thus cutting the time needed to respond.

Automate the processes for requesting brochures, subscribing to newsletters and signing up for events

Not every email needs to be replied to in person. Make sure that prospective students can subscribe to email updates and sign up for events without human intervention. This can cut volume of enquiries substantially and ensures that your team interacts with the most serious prospective students.

Inadequate capture of contact details

Because deciding where to study is a process, not an event, it's important that enough people opt in to receive further information. Many university websites are not set up to obtain opt-ins. Thus, while the site may get many visitors, few opt to stay updated. How can you obtain the contact details of more prospective students?

1. **Give a strong reason why**, for example, "To be invited to future events".
2. Then **simply ask**, for example, by having a "Stay updated" button on every page and adding an additional newsletter opt-in tick box to contact forms.

Uncertainty about privacy laws

It's often assumed privacy laws such as General Data Protection Regulation (GDPR) forbid sending promotional messages and retargeting website visitors with banners or advertisements on social platforms. However, there is hardly anything that cannot be done, so long as you get informed consent from the person whose personal information you store.

Here an example, though not from the field of education, about how far this can go. My son has a rare kidney condition and was asked to participate in a study by Radboud University. We had to go through many pages of documentation to understand what the study was about and how it would be conducted, and this was followed up by a call from the researcher. In the end we consented to almost everything they asked for. This included allowing a DNA sample to be collected, stored for 10 years, and shared (in anonymised format) within and outside the EU.

My wife and I gave our consent because we understood the relevance and value of the study to society, and possibly even to our own son.

Before you ask for consent for your follow-up campaign, ask yourself what's in it for prospective students. And make sure these benefits are communicated clearly to prospective students at the point where you request consent.

7.2 WAYS TO FOLLOW UP

Here are the most common ways to stay in touch with prospective students after they've visited your website:

- email newsletters,
- remarketing,
- phone calls.

Email newsletters

These newsletters are a classic and can still be effective, provided the messages are well crafted. As with all forms of communication, the key is to connect with prospective students and to find out where they are in their process. A common pitfall is talking too much about yourself, instead of connecting with what's going on in their minds.

Writing good email copy is time consuming. That's why I recommend setting up an on-boarding sequence. This is a series of well-crafted emails that are sent to new subscribers after they sign up for the newsletter. Over a period of a few weeks, this sequence can cover all the different subjects they might be wondering about.

You create the copy for this sequence once and review them every year. Everyone who signs up will receive these messages. It's okay if the emails become less frequent after the on-boarding sequence has run out. In fact, they could be limited to invitations to events and reminders that the application deadline is approaching.

Remarketing

While email newsletters work well for the most engaged prospective students, not everyone will open their email. And only a fraction of website visitors will subscribe to the newsletter in the first place. Remarketing is a form of web advertising. It's surprisingly cheap, because it targets only the people who have visited your website. With remarketing, your messages can appear on banners across the Internet and in visitors' social feeds. You can set up different messages to show one, three, six and seven days after a visit. This prevents the follow-up from becoming annoying and allows you to highlight different angles.

7.1 An example of a remarketing ad.

A good remarketing ad campaign has to be set up carefully, but once it starts, it more or less runs by itself since you're only showing the ads to people who have recently interacted with your website. The same set of ads is shown; it's the audience that changes. The small size of the audience also means that remarketing advertising campaigns can be run on a very limited advertising budget. Once or twice a year you might want to review whether the ad graphics and copy are still up to date.

If you plan to do remarketing, make sure to display to new website visitors a cookie notification that gives them the option to opt out of marketing cookies.

Phone calls

You may or may not have the resources to follow up with a personal phone call to every prospective student. It's effective but generally done only with high-ticket programmes, such as Executive MBAs.

However, why not pick the 10%–20% most promising prospective students and give them a personal call? Besides raising the chance of the person enrolling, it's also a great way to learn about the motivations of prospective students and to be able to answer any questions that might not be covered sufficiently on the website.

7.3 CONCLUSION

After all the effort spent on attracting people to your website and educating them, don't drop the ball in the follow-up stage! Choosing where to study is a process, not an event. That's why it's important that universities stay in touch with prospective students.

Be transparent about what prospective students sign up for, and make sure that every message provides value. It's hardly ever feasible to follow up on a one-by-one basis. Fortunately, CRMs, email marketing programmes and advertising platforms can empower universities to send out personalised follow-up messages at scale.

SECTION II

PUTTING SEARCH ADS TO WORK

Now that we have drawn an overall picture of the different parts that make up an online student recruitment strategy, it's time to get our hands dirty and set up that SEA campaign!

As a tool in a marketer's tool-kit, Google Ads enters the picture in the attraction stage. They are particularly well suited to reaching prospective students who are fairly close to enrolling, who already have some idea of which programme they are interested in pursuing.

In the chapters of this section, I'll go step-by-step, covering how to get the best bang for your buck with Google Ads.

For detailed videos and updates about the latest developments, I encourage you to subscribe to my newsletter updates at guusgoorts.com.

8

Types of search campaigns

In chapter 5, about attraction, I divided outreach campaigns into search, broad outreach and early outreach. In this chapter we'll dive deeper into the different types of search campaigns that can be distinguished on the basis of the approach employed:

- branded,
- course-based,
- competition-based, and
- foreign-language.

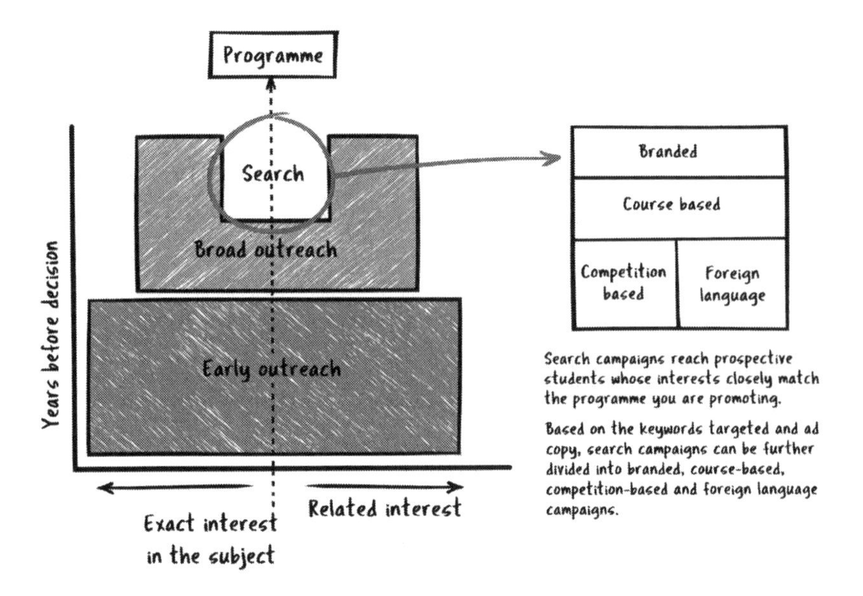

8.1 Search campaigns can be further subdivided by approach.

8.1 BRANDED CAMPAIGNS

AB University Business School Online | Award-Winning Faculty

Ad online.abu.edu/

Discover our world-class faculty and experience edge-of-your-seat online learning. Real ABU professors. Real ABU cases. Master the skills needed for real-world success. Unique Online Programs. Apply for Free. Case-Based Learning. Online Courses. World-Class Content.

8.2 Branded search campaigns can give specific programmes more exposure.

Branded search campaigns show their ads when someone searches for a specific brand. If you're AB University and someone searches for "AB University Open Day", your branded campaign may kick in and show an ad that leads straight to the open day registration page.

Strong points

- **Make it easy to sign up**. Unlike organic search results, search ads allow you to determine exactly what people see when they search. If the open day registration page is tucked away on your website, this is a great way to clearly signpost it.
- **Accompany traditional campaigns**. A search campaign goes together with other campaigns on the radio or TV, or in print. It can also be used with campaigns conducted outdoors or through PR activities. People may have heard about your event on the radio and then search for it. Branded search campaigns make sure these people are led straight to the right page on your website.
- **Defend against competitors using your brand name**. By running an ad with your own brand name, you'll make sure you'll always show up first when someone searches for your institution name. This holds even when competitors target your brand name.
- **Inflate conversion statistics**. Branded campaigns show the highest conversion rates at the lowest cost per lead. They are directed at people who have already been persuaded elsewhere. If there were no ads, they might have come through an organic search. So it's important to take the results of a branded campaign with a grain of salt and not to attach too much value to large numbers of conversions.

Weaker points

- **Reach new people?** Branded campaigns hinge on your existing reputation and brand recognition. You make it easier for people who already know you to find what they want. This is valuable. But don't expect to reach new audiences.

- **Let you advertise on a tight budget?** While the CPC is relatively low, there will be a lot of clicks. Most of the clicks will be from people who would have otherwise clicked the organic search result, which is free.

To sum up, branded campaigns can make things easier for people who were already looking for your institution. If you're on a tight budget, leave this type of campaign aside and focus on making sure your website is easy to navigate when people access it through organic searches.

8.2 COURSE-BASED CAMPAIGNS

Nursing Degree | University of Phoenix® Online Ad
Ad www.phoenix.edu
Enroll for Your Nursing Degree Online. Flexible Schedules to Fit any Lifestyle! Built for Working Adults. Degree program: RN to BSN, BS in Health Admin, Masters in Nursing.

8.3 An example of a course-based ad.

Course-based campaigns show ads based on keywords related to the programme they are looking for. So if you offer a bachelor in chemistry, ads for course-based campaigns will show for keywords such as "chemistry degree" and "study chemistry".

Strong points

- **Reach new prospective students**. Course-based campaigns are great for reaching people who don't know about you but are looking to study a subject for which you offer programmes.
- **Advertise with tight budgets**. With these campaigns you can move the needle for specific programmes, even if you have a fairly limited budget,

In short, course-based campaigns are highly targeted. The CPC is usually high, but the people who click are exactly the type of people you want to reach out to. In most cases you will want to begin with a course-based campaign.

8.3 COMPETITION-BASED CAMPAIGNS

Distance Learning University | Study Your Degree At Home | abu.edu

Study From Home In Africa, No Visa Required, Browse Course & Apply Now!

8.4 AB University could run this ad in Zimbabwe so that it would be seen by people there who search for any one of a large number of foreign universities.

Imagine that you are promoting a distance learning programme for a college that isn't that well known. You know that many prospective students in Zimbabwe have the ambition to study abroad and are searching for "Harvard University", even though they may not obtain a visa. A competition-based ad will show up when a prospective student searches for a phrase like "Harvard University". The ad copy will emphasise the specific advantages of your programme over the competition (no visa required, in this case) and point the searcher to the programme page.

Strong point

- **Broaden your reach**. Competition-based campaigns can reach prospective students who are a good match for your programme but might not know about you.

Weaker point

- **Some competitors may take offense**. Some of your competitors may also be your partners. If you run ads that show when people search for their brand name, you may need to be careful not to offend them.

8.4 FOREIGN-LANGUAGE CAMPAIGNS

Medienmanagement studieren |
Download unsere Broschüre Anzeige
Ad www.nhlstenden.com/Bachelor/M...
Internationales Studium mit anerkanntem Bachelor Abschluss in Holland. Auf Englisch studieren.

8.5 Ad in German, run in Germany, for a programme delivered in English in the Netherlands.

If your goal is to recruit students abroad, why not run ads in other languages? Even if your degree is taught in English, you'll reach vastly more students in specific countries (and their parents) if you deliver the ads in their language.

Strong point

- **Dig deeper into one country**. If your internationalisation strategy has specific target countries, campaigns in those countries' languages will reach vastly more prospective students. While they might not have searched using English keywords, some of them will be open to studying in English.

Weaker point

- **It's a lot of work**. It's not just about keywords and ad copy: you'll also need to have landing pages and essential web content available in that language. Ideally, you'll have student ambassadors or staff available to answer queries in the language of the campaign.

In short, foreign-language campaigns are great if you are committed to certain target countries and want to deepen your reach there.

8.5 CONCLUSION

This chapter has provided an overview of the different types of search campaign and when they come in.

To make the most out of your advertising budget, it generally makes sense to implement the campaigns one by one, in this order:

1. course-based,
2. branded,
3. competition-based,
4. foreign-language.

9

Putting everything together

THUS FAR WE HAVE covered the context that is needed for a successful search advertising programme. We're getting close to actually implementing the search campaign. In this chapter we will apply all the points made in the previous chapter.

9.1 CALCULATE YOUR EXPECTED RETURN

Decisions on how to spend large media budgets are too often made based on intuition. While this was perhaps justified in the past, today **the results that can be expected from a given advertising budget are perfectly knowable**, albeit with a margin of error.

Before going any further, **you should know** what can reasonably be expected. In many cases – especially if there is no urgent short-term need – your budget will be better invested in other forms of online marketing, such as SEO. Too often, the decision to go ahead with search advertising is made without sufficient forethought: "Let's just start and see what happens!"

Before embarking on any campaign, do the following exercise. It may lead you to change your budget or even to use the budget for something else.

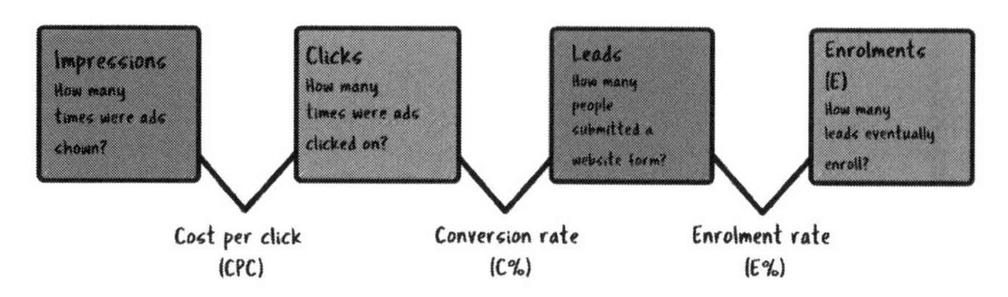

9.1 Overview of how the various campaign metrics fit together from first impression to enrolment.

Bear in mind that people search for degrees one to two years before actually enrolling. So what is your growth goal for a particular degree in two years' time? And what percentage of this increase do you hope to bring in through search advertising? Starting from this goal, you can work backwards to your budget. The formula for estimating the required budget is

$$\$=(E \times CPC) \div (C\% \times E\%)$$

Symbol	What is it?	How do I get this figure?
$	Estimated budget required	The amount you estimate you'll spend in advertising fees paid to Google. This is either the number you want to calculate or a given.
E	Enrolment target	How many additional enrolments do you want to obtain two years from now from search advertising in the interim period?
CPC	Estimated average cost per click	Keyword tools such as Ubersuggest (free) and SEMrush (paid) give information on the number of searches and estimated CPC by keyword and target country.
C%	Conversion rate	This refers to the proportion of website visitors that become leads by filling out a form or contacting you in another way. If you keep track of conversions in Google Analytics, it will calculate this number for you.
E%	Enrolment rate	This is the total number of enrolments for the programme last year divided by the total number of leads generated for that same programme in the same year.

The variables $ and E are quite simple: they represent the amount you expect to spend and the number of enrolments you expect to achieve. I'll now discuss the other variables in more detail.

CPC

This is what you will end up paying Google on average for one click on an ad. If you've run search campaigns before, this figure is **readily available** in your **Google Ads account**. This is definitely the most reliable way to estimate this cost.

If this is new to you, you can get a **decent estimate** using a **keyword tool**. I personally like SEMrush, but there are many options. When you provide both a keyword you aim to target and the target country, SEMrush will give you a number of related keywords and the CPC for each. For example, for a chemistry degree in the USA, the expected CPC works out to be $4.15.

PHRASE MATCH KEYWORDS (28)

Keyword	Volume	CPC (€)
chemistry degree	720	4.15

9.2 This screenshot from SEMrush indicates the search volume and CPC for a particular keyword.

Conversion rate

As mentioned above, the conversion rate is the number of website leads divided by the total number of website visitors. If you have set up goal tracking in Google Analytics (more about that in the next chapter), it will give you this number.

Using a simple example, we can illustrate how to calculate the conversion rate. If 1,000 website visits generate 25 leads, the conversion rate will be 25 ÷ 1000 = 0.025 or 2.5%.

Enrolment rate

As already mentioned, the enrolment rate can be calculated by dividing the number of enrolments in a given year by the number of leads. For example, if 50 people enrolled in your chemistry degree programme last year, and 300 people enquired about it, your enrolment rate will be 50 ÷ 300 = 0.167 or 16.7%.

Sample calculation

To continue with the illustrative examples already used, let's say you want an additional 10 enrolments for the chemistry degree you're marketing in the USA. How would you calculate the estimated budget required?

- **$:** This is what we want to calculate
- **E:** 10 additional students
- **CPC:** $4.15
- **E%:** 16.5%
- **C%:** 2.5%

Filling it all in, we get the following:

$=(E x CPC) ÷ (E% x C%) = (10 x 4.15) ÷ (0.165 x 0.025) = $10,060

Thus, the required budget to recruit an additional 10 students for our chemistry degree would be $10,000. That means allocating $1,000 of your ad budget for each additional enrolled student. Keep in mind that these new students won't all materialise within the first year. And campaign management expenses and/or time spent managing the campaign have not been accounted for yet.
If you manage to recruit 10 additional enrolees, with an ad spend of $1,000 each, will it be considered a success? If so, go for it! If not, see if there is a way to improve these numbers. How? Read on.

9.2 IMPROVE YOUR EXPECTED RETURN

As you can see above, cost per enrolment is a function of a number of variables. You can cut the required budget in half by doing one of the following things:

- cutting **CPC** in half,
- doubling **C%** (conversion rate), or
- doubling **E%** (enrolment rate).

If you can improve each of these three figures a bit, or do more than one of the above, you can stack the improvement and cut the budget in half, and then halve it again. What are the possibilities?

CPC

Search ads are very competitive. They reach the right people at exactly the right time, and it's no surprise that everyone wants in on the game. You can lower your CPC in several ways:

- Choose target keywords and countries strategically.
- Check the exact search terms that people used, and exclude irrelevant ones as "negative keywords".
- Focus on countries or areas with a lower CPC, if this option is available to you.
- See if people are searching in other languages and if keywords for those languages are cheaper.
- Make sure your keywords, ad copy and landing page content match. Google greatly rewards well-executed campaigns (more about this in the next chapter).

Conversion rate

In our chemistry degree example, the website conversion rate is only 2.5% and thus low. Imagine it could be 10%. That would reduce the required ad budget by 75%! There are certain common causes of low conversion rates:

- **Friction in the enquiry process.** Forms might be hard to find or have too many required fields. Both of these features discourage enquiries.
- **Lack of a clear call to action**. The landing page may not make it clear what the visitor needs to do.
- **Too much information.** If the landing page has too much information, it may overwhelm prospective students or take away their reason for asking questions or downloading a brochure.
- **Landing pages that aren't mobile friendly**. These will quickly leave mobile users discouraged.

The question is, can you identify any of the above issues on your own website, and is your organisation willing to tackle them before embarking on a Google Ads campaign? Setting up dedicated landing pages for the campaign is often the fastest way to fix the issues listed above. It's always better to improve the entire website. But if this can't get done, setting up dedicated landing pages for your campaign will help you avoid having to wait until a new website is up and running, which can take years.

Tools like Unbounce (unbounce.com) and InstaPage (instapage.com) allow you to quickly stir up a new landing page and easily make modifications on the fly. Although it takes longer, you can also build a page from scratch. In some cases restrictions imposed by your institution will force you to go this way.

So how can a better landing page improve your campaign? Let's run the same numbers again, but this time with the following assumptions:

- The conversion rate has improved from 2.5% to 10%.
- The one-time cost of setting up a better landing page is $1,000.

In this example, we end up with a total campaign cost of $3,500, or $350 per enrolled student – down from $1,000 per enrolled student.

Enrolment rate

In a similar vein, you can improve your enrolment rate. If this is below 20%, I'd look for ways to improve it. On average, prospective students are not likely to get in touch with more than five institutions. Ask yourself whether you are

- communicating clearly who your ideal student is,
- making clear why prospective students should care about your course offering,inviting leads to events and webinars on a regular basis,
- making it easy to get in touch with reach staff and student ambassadors, and
- replying promptly to all enquiries.

9.3 CONCLUSION

Before deciding whether to run a new search campaign, calculate the expected results (or required budget). This can help identify bottlenecks before you have spent considerable amounts of money on Google Ads.

Going through this process will help you avoid the "leaky bucket" problem, where you spend a lot on paid traffic from Google but have most of the traffic "leak" away once it reaches your website.

10

Measure your results

In the previous chapter we covered the planning that needs to happen ahead of your search advertising campaign to ensure you get the result that can be expected for a given budget. Once the campaign is up and running, you'll need to **check your metrics regularly** to know whether you're on track. In this way, if you're not, you'll still have time to make adjustments.

In this chapter, I cover the steps to be taken to accurately capture the metrics you need to stay in control of your campaign while it runs and to identify any gaps in your recruitment process when the campaign ends. In Chapter 4 I mentioned the most important metrics for measuring campaign success:

1. cost per lead (CPL),
2. lead engagement,
3. percentage of applicants,
4. offers made,
5. and students who enrolled.

The first metric is quite different from the other four, so I'll start by discussing the *why* and *how* of tracking metric 1 and then go on to metrics 2–5.

10.1 METRIC 1: CPL

Why is CPL relevant?

CPL is absolutely crucial for keeping your campaign under control. It is the bridge between your campaign management and your overall strategy. If the CPL is too high, you know you won't achieve your goal for the targeted number of leads. So when the alarm sounds, you need to act immediately to bring the campaign back under control.

As mentioned in Chapter 4, CPL is calculated by dividing the total campaign cost by the number of leads acquired through the campaign. If it's too high, one of two things is happening:

1. you're **paying too much** for single clicks, or
2. you're **converting too few clicks into leads** on your website.

The root cause of both may lie in your SEA campaign (irrelevant targeting, a lack of compelling ad copy or incorrect URLs) or on your webpage (content is not compelling or is badly matched to the SEA campaign, it's hard to submit enquiries, or there are issues with mobile use).

What's neat is that you can **get the CPL from your Google Ads account**, and this will help you see which ad copy and keywords work well and which don't. In fact, when you have this information, Google can do most of the optimisation work for you.

How do you measure CPL?

First, define all the actions that prospective students can take to get in touch with you when they visit your website. This can include

- filling out a form (e.g. to enquire, download a brochure or sign up for an open day),
- participating in an online chat,
- making a phone call.

Every time one of these contact moments happens, Google Analytics needs to receive a signal that the conversion has taken place. You do this by **setting up conversion tracking**. (I won't run through the step-by-step process here, as I'm sure Google will do a much better job of keeping this information up-to-date on its support website.[1]). Second, you need to link your Google Analytics property to your Google Ads account[2] and import your analytics goals.[3]

To summarise, CPL is the one crucial metric you need to know while running your campaign, and this requires some set-up beforehand.

10.2 METRICS 2–5: LEAD ENGAGEMENT, PERCENTAGE OF APPLICANTS, OFFERS GIVEN, OFFERS ACCEPTED – STUDENTS WHO ENROLLED

Why are these metrics relevant?

As mentioned earlier in this book, recruitment is a process. These metrics are essential for evaluating campaigns after they have ended, identifying gaps in the overall recruitment process and making improvements year after year.

1 https://support.google.com/google-ads/answer/1722054
2 https://support.google.com/google-ads/answer/1704341
3 https://support.google.com/google-ads/answer/2375435

How do you calculate them?

Metrics 2–5 can only be calculated after some time has passed, as prospective students go through their decision-making process, encouraged by your follow-up.

To calculate these metrics, you need to do two things:

1. **Capture the lead source** upon first contact.
2. **Keep track of leads over time**, preferably with a CRM.

The question of how to keep track of leads over time in a CRM is highly specific to each institution, and discussing it would probably take up an entire book itself. Here I'll focus on capturing the lead source each time contact is made. If you do this consistently, you'll have the raw material to calculate these metrics.

To be able to calculate each of these five metrics later on, you need to capture one piece of information right at the moment a prospective student fills in a form, starts a chat or makes a phone call: **the lead source**. You can do this using hidden fields. On the surface, your form may look like this:

The prospective student just fills in the basics. There are however, a few invisible fields added in the back end of the form. These may include the following:

- **IP address.** This can be used to determine which country the enquiry came from.
- **Source.** This is the website the visitor came from before landing on your website.

- **Medium**. This refers to the type of traffic involved, for example, *"CPC"* for per-click advertising, *referral* for visitors who clicked links on other sites and *organic* for organic searches.
- **Campaign**. This specifies the specific campaign that brought the visitor to your site (e.g. *bachelor-business*).
- **URL from which the enquiry was submitted**. This often provides additional context for any questions asked.

10.1 Example of an enquiry form.

There are two ways of obtaining this source data at the point of submission:

- **Through direct integration with Google Analytics**. This takes a good deal of development work as Google isn't very keen on this data being taken out of its ecosystem. A third-party program that can help with this is GA Connector.[4] It is the preferred method because it will attach a source to *all* your traffic and not just to the traffic from your paid campaigns.

- **Through tagging your URLs**. This is your next best option if you can't pull off direct integration with Google Analytics (yet). In the URL of each of your ads, you can add extra parameters such as the campaign name. These are much easier to capture in forms. There are many tools that can help you build tracking URLs.[5]

When a prospective student submits the form, the page fills in these hidden fields and then sends the data along with the information that prospective students have already filled in. As this source data consistently gets recorded and you record future engagements in your CRM, you will be able to trace how many of your leads showed up on your open day (lead engagement) or eventually enrolled (offers made).

10.3 CONCLUSION

In Chapter 4, I discussed the role of analytics in your recruitment process in making sure every aspect of your process is under control. The current section has shown how to capture the key data points needed to calculate all essential ratios so that you can steer your analytics campaign. Of course, there are countless tools and technologies for tracking your data. I'll keep up with them on guusgoorts.com.

---

4 https://gaconnector.com/

5 For example, https://ga-dev-tools.appspot.com/campaign-url-builder/

11

Campaign set-up: keywords

Up to this point I've covered everything that should happen before and after prospective students see your ad and click it: from strategy to analytics and follow-up. Now it's time to get our hands dirty and set up the actual search advertising campaign. In the following chapters we'll trace the steps prospective students take as they experience your campaign:

1. keywords,
2. ad copy,
3. landing pages.

In this chapter I'll focus on keywords. They are the foundation of every search campaign and ultimately determine who is going to see your ads. Get your keywords right and you'll be aiming at the right group of people: those who intend to enrol in a programme your institution offers.

To include the right keywords in your campaign, you need to do keyword research. This can be divided into four phases:

1. brainstorm,
2. analyse,
3. categorise,
4. prioritise.

11.1 KEYWORD BRAINSTORMING

The goal of keyword research is to generate a list of potential keywords that cover as much ground as possible. In Chapter 8, I broke down search campaigns into four different types:

1. branded search,
2. course-based,
3. competition-based,
4. foreign-language.

Each has its own set of typical keywords that generally work, and these are the best starting point for brainstorming relevant terms.

Branded search

The typical search phrases are as follows:

[your institution name]
[your institution name] + [course name]

Course-based

Which programmes do you intend to promote? Based on the subject, the following keywords usually work well.

Phrases of three words or more

[programme name] + [degree, bachelor, master, etc.] + [city or country]
For example, *mathematics bachelor Brussels*

Two-word phrases

[programme name] + [degree / course / bachelor / master / school / university]
For example, *economics degree* or *business university*

Single term (one word) (subject only)

[programme name]
For example, *mathematics*

The longer the keyword, the surer you can be about the searcher's intent. But fewer people will use longer keywords in searches.

Competition-based

If you're a university marketer, you know which institutions are your main competitors. Write down their names. You can add their brand names to your campaign and also "spy" on their campaigns to see which keywords they focus on (more on this later).

Foreign-language

If you're planning to recruit students in other countries, you can repeat the course-based brainstorm but for keywords in another language and in this way come up with a separate set of keywords.

11.2 KEYWORD ANALYSIS

After you have compiled a long list of potential keywords, the next step is to analyse them with a keyword tool.[6] This tool can help you identify related keywords that you haven't thought about. It can also give you more information about each keyword phrase: the expected CPC and estimated monthly search volume.

Here are the steps I recommend:

1. Plug in the keywords you have come up with so far into a keyword tool, and it will suggest many related keywords that you might not have thought of. Add these additional keywords to your list. And take note of the estimated CPC and volume for each keyword.
2. Plug in the URLs of each of your competitors. See which keywords they are targeting. If you find any that are relevant and that you haven't thought of, note them down.
3. You'll also come across mismatches: keywords that are not relevant for the programmes that you plan to advertise but closely resemble your keywords. For example, people may be looking for
   - *free mathematics master,*
   - *logistics bachelor scholarships, or*
   - *online language course.*

6 There are many such tools available. Google offers its own tool in its ad interface, but restricts the data there and doesn't allow "spying" on the competition. I highly recommend using a third-party tool, of which many are available. I personally love SEMrush, which requires a subscription. A free alternative is Ubersuggest.

If you don't offer free or online programmes or don't have any scholarships available for specific programmes, place on a "negative" list the words that make these keywords irrelevant. This list will contain all the keywords that you *don't* want to trigger your ads. Based on the examples above, you could add "*free*", "*scholarships*" and "*online*" to your negative list. As long as a search query contains any term that is on the negative list, Google will not display your ad. This saves ad budget and prevents potentially irrelevant enquiries.

When you have completed the steps above, you'll have a long list of potential keyword phrases along with the estimated CPC and search volumes for each. And you'll also have a list of negative keywords.

11.3 KEYWORD CATEGORISATION

In this step you sort the keywords into groups of closely related phrases. This will help ensure that your ad copy is **matched exactly** to the keyword being searched for. Each of these tightly knit groups of keywords forms an **ad group** and has its own ad copy. Moreover, the link in the ad can go to a specific web page.

This enables you to offer searchers exactly the ad copy and landing page that they were looking for. Here are some things to keep in mind:

- Never mix keywords for different programmes or campaign types in the same ad group.
- For course-based campaigns, always have separate ad groups for keywords that contain "*bachelor*", "*master*", and "*university*" or "*school*".

11.4 KEYWORD PRIORITISATION

Your campaign budget may be large or small, but it won't be unlimited. To maximise the outcome of any advertising budget, you need to start with the keywords that signify the highest level of interest ("intent") with the searcher, and then, as budget allows, gradually broaden the campaign.

What's the "right size" for your campaign? You'll never know for sure, and that's okay: you can fine-tune it along the way.

Here is how you can make an initial estimate:

1. Look at the spreadsheet you last touched in Step 2 ("expand") and make a rough estimate of the average CPC across your keywords. Let's say that this is €2.
2. Now take your monthly budget (say, €1,000) and divide it by this average CPC. You now know you can afford roughly 500 clicks per month.
3. Assuming a click through rate of 5%, this means you need to get 500 x 20 = 10,000 impressions to fully utilise your budget.
4. Go back to your spreadsheet and figure which target keywords will add up to about 10,000 impressions. I recommend prioritising keywords in the following order:
   - course-based (three words or longer)
   - course-based (two words)
   - competition-based
   - foreign-language (if relevant)
   - branded
   - course-based (single word)

Match types

Beware: Google can take a lot of liberty as to whether a keyword you added matches a user's search query. This can be a good thing, because it's impossible to imagine every possible search phrase, but it can also cause wasted budget.

For example, if you are advertising a French language school, you might have added the keyword phrase

french language school

If you don't add any limitations, the keyword phrase is called a "broad match". Google will deem the phrase "*french cooking school*" to be a good enough match, even though it's irrelevant..

You can prevent this by inserting the "(+)" sign in front of each of the words in the query, which is called "*modified broad match*"[7]. This will limit Google to only display your ad if the specific words behind a "(+)" sign are part of the searcher's query. So you'll note down:

+french +language +school

With this modified broad match keyword, your ads can show when someone searches for "*french language school paris*" but not when someone searches "french cooking school", because the latter query does not include the required word "language".

7 For a more in-depth explanation about match types, you can refer to https://support.google.com/google-ads/answer/7478529?hl=en

I generally use only modified broad matches at the start, supplemented by a strong negative keyword list, and then finetune this when the campaign is running.

11.5 CONCLUSION

When setting up a Google Search campaign, the first step is to identify the keywords you want the campaign to target. This determines who gets to see your ad.

In this chapter I have covered the brainstorm phase and how to narrow down the long list of keywords that comes out of it and then to divide them into ad groups made up of closely related keywords. In the next chapter, I'll discuss how to write great ads for each of these groups.

12

Campaign set-up: ad copy

THE NEXT THING YOU need for a killer campaign is **compelling** and **relevant ad copy**. Too often, ad copy is an afterthought and left to whoever happens to set up the campaign. But if your ad doesn't set you apart, chances are that prospective students will never even click it and learn more about you.

Writing good ad copy is like a doing puzzle: you have to fit all the pieces together.

1. Focus on the **unique selling points** of your school, city and programme.
2. Make sure there is a **good match between each keyword and the ad copy** it triggers.
3. Ensure that **ad copy matches the landing page**. The ad should provide a seamless transition to the landing page that comes up when people click on it;
4. **Test** whether your brilliant copy ideas actually work in practice.
5. Comply with **character limits.**

Let's examine points 1–4 in detail.

12.1 UNIQUE SELLING POINTS

To know what to emphasise, you need to know what prospective students are looking for. Here are some of the ways you can find out:

- Go out and speak with current students in the programme.
- Pose as a prospective student (or parent) and enquire with other institutions and your own.
- Search for reviews about yourself and competitors on comparison websites and forums.
- Put yourself in the shoes of a prospective student and research your options, forgetting about what you already know. What information comes your way?

In the end you should **come up with three unique selling points** that you want to get across for each programme. These will take centre stage in your ad copy, as well as on your landing page and in other communications.

Phrase your unique selling points as **specific facts**. Avoid general claims. Everyone can claim to have a great environment for learning or a diverse student population. The ad becomes much more compelling when you say that your students represent "82 nationalities".

The following screenshot shows the difference between real differentiators and clichés.

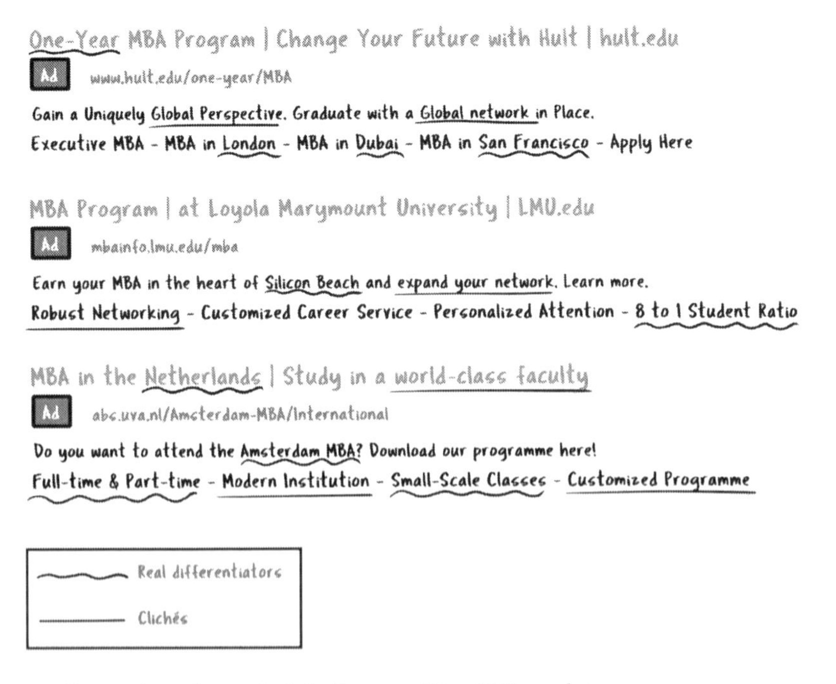

12.1 Comparison of several ads in the competitive MBA market.

12.2 KEYWORD/AD COPY FIT

Even if your campaign is geared to promoting only one programme, your keywords should be sorted into separate ad groups and the **ad copy** should be **adjusted to fit** with the keywords in the group in question. Every new ad group means extra work, but it's well worth it. When your ad corresponds directly to the search phrase that the prospective student has entered, a higher percentage of searchers will click the ad. This clickthrough-rate (CTR) is an important signal to Google about the campaign's quality. A high CTR will lower the campaign's CPC tremendously and give your ads more exposure.

For example, let's say you're promoting your Bachelor of Fashion Design. You could sort your keywords into these groups:

- *Fashion courses,*
- *Fashion degree,*
- *Fashion design,*
- *Fashion marketing.*

Consider the ad in Figure 12.2. Why does it work well?

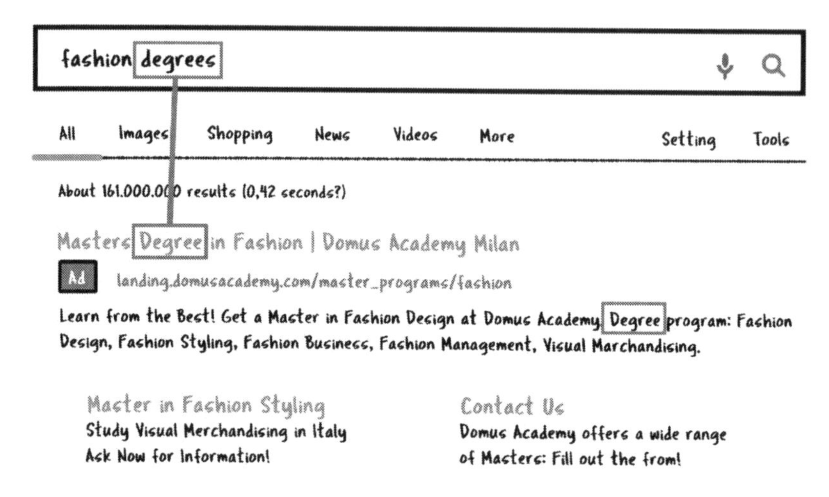

12.2 It's vital that the keywords a particular prospective student searches for appear prominently in the ad.

Here's why:

1. People are more likely to click an ad that contains **the same words** they searched for. So the ad is likely to have a better click-through rate.
2. **Google recognises that this is a relevant ad and awards it with extra exposure.** Google awards ad positions based on a combination of your bid and the ad's relevance (e.g. is the keyword in the ad copy?). Even if you have the budget, you can't buy your way to a high position if your ad copy isn't highly relevant.

3. **Different keywords signal a (slightly) different intention**. To illustrate, someone who is looking for a degree will be looking to study long term. People searching for "courses" may be looking for shorter-term, professional-development kinds of options. If you can address this in your ad copy and subsequent landing page, you'll speak much better to what prospective students are actually searching for.

You might think that this is a lot of work for just a few clicks. And that's absolutely true. The thing is, the **few** people in Europe who search for "fashion management courses" in a given week are **exactly** the **motivated prospective students** who are going to decide very soon which degree they'll enrol in. In student recruitment we need high-quality clicks, not so much high volumes.

12.3 AD COPY/LANDING PAGE FIT

Have you ever clicked on an ad with anticipation, only to be disappointed that what was promised in the ad wasn't delivered? To get a good fit between keyword and ad copy, you'll write lots of different ads. If you do this well, taking cues from the keywords, you'll write ad copy that emphasises a variety of points.

Keep in mind that the ad still needs to fit with the page to which it directs people who click it. If the copy is different, you may need to link the ad to a different page. You may even need to set up a new landing page so that people who click the ad will find exactly what they have been led to expect.

12.4 ALWAYS BE TESTING

In the steps just discussed, you have taken great care to come up with great, relevant copy that resonates with your prospective students. Testing is where the rubber meets the road. Unlike traditional media, Google gives you almost real-time feedback on what works in the form of CTR and conversion rates.

Don't create just one ad for each ad group. Write four variations that differ from one another in real ways. Here are some strategies for creating varied ads:

- Emphasise different unique selling points in each.
- Phrase the same benefit in completely different ways.
- Use different calls to action.
- Experiment with sentence order.

If you have two ads active at any one time, you'll see that one will get a higher click-through rate and/or gather more filled-in enquiry forms. Once there is a clear winner, pause the losing ad and activate yet another to see if it can beat the previous winner. This way you're constantly sharpening your ability to interest people in your programmes. This process is called A/B testing. Google Ads actively encourages it, but it's practiced far too little.

You may find that certain unique selling points trigger a lot more interest than others. This is not just useful for getting people to click your ads. You can take what you learn from testing ad copy and use this throughout your communication efforts: in print, on the website, in open days and so on.

Google has options that automatically rotate and test ads. I'd advise against using them when starting out – there is too much to learn. When you've learned what makes your ads tick and have gotten rid of any ads that have proven to be ineffective, it's certainly a good option to let Google do the work.

12.5 CONCLUSION

The overriding goal of good ad copy is to persuade people to click on the ad and find out more. In this chapter we covered the essentials of creating good ad copy: unique selling points that are genuine and specific, a good fit between the ad copy and (1) the keywords that triggered the ad and (2) the page that follows when the ad is clicked, and continuous testing.

In the next chapter, we'll follow our prospective student to the next step: the landing page.

13

Campaign set-up: landing pages

After clicking your ad, the next thing prospective students see is the landing page. The term "landing page" refers to the specific page website visitors "land on" when they click an ad. It can be a page that has been specifically set up for the advertising campaign or a page on an existing website. Many people do not consider landing pages part of the search campaign, but if a campaign doesn't work, it's very often the landing page that is to blame.

A great landing page is

1. mobile-friendly,
2. focused,
3. trustworthy, and
4. action oriented.

I'll now consider each of these points in detail.

13.1 MOBILE-FRIENDLY

Depending on the target country, you can expect 60-70% of the prospective students to access the landing page through their mobile phone. Visitors using mobiles will lose interest if they come to a page that is hard for them to read. Beyond this, Google will hold back your ads from mobile searchers. Thus, a portion of your target market may not even get to see your ads.

What if your school website isn't mobile-friendly yet? Do you have a new website that is in the works but will take another year to complete? In these cases, you have two options:

1. **Don't advertise at all.** Seriously, don't waste your money.
2. **Set up a separate page.** With tools like Unbounce and Instapage, you can set up a special, mobile-friendly page on a subdomain of your website.

Setting up a separate page is never my first choice. But it's often the only option that is feasible in the short term.

13.2 FOCUSED

Landing pages should provide additional relevant information that is a natural extension of the ad. They should have clear headings so that anyone viewing them can get the main points quickly. Searchers are often impatient, so don't test their patience!

The most important question the landing page should answer is "Why should I care?" You should address this question directly, using headings such as

- Why choose this programme?
- Is this degree for you?

Try to convey your message in as few words as possible. Avoid long overviews of everything that is going to be covered during the programme! This may be very important to the faculty members, but your prospective student doesn't know enough about the field to understand the significance of all this. If they did, they wouldn't be applying for the programme. So keep to the big picture:

- **Why choose us** (and not a similar programme at another university)?
- What will the **experience** of studying at our university and in our city be like?
- How does this programme prepare you for your **professional future**?

13.3 TRUSTWORTHY

The landing page also needs to build trust. The best way of doing this is through social proof: what others say about you carries much more weight than what you say about yourself. Social proof can take various forms.

Accreditations. Does your school have accreditations, such as AACSB accreditation for business schools? Make sure they are mentioned prominently, with a short line explaining what they stand for.

Rankings. We all know the QS rankings, but there are many more (inter)national rankings. Did the programme, or your school, do well in any rankings or reviews? Make sure it's mentioned with a badge and some explanation of what the ranking means.

Testimonials. It's important for prospective students to see that others they can relate to have chosen the programme and are happy with their choice. Aim for a few reviews, perhaps four. Each should cover different aspects of your institution, and the group of reviewing students should be as diverse as possible in terms of gender, ethnicity and nationality.

Video. Don't overdo it, but one well-made video showing your institution's people and buildings can do a great job in making the programme a lot more tangible.

Statistics. Do you have labour market statistics that make you look good? Include them on the landing page.

13.4 ACTION ORIENTED

It's easy to lose your way as you explain how great a programme is and describe all the options that prospective students will have down the road. But landing pages should have only one goal: **to lead the visitor to the next step**.

If a prospective student merely views the page and leaves, they are likely to forget everything within a day or two. Landing pages should be designed to bring visitors across the threshold of contacting the institution for the first time.

If the page is focused, builds trust, is easy to use and mobile-friendly, prospective students may take the next step. Consider these additional tips on how to inspire them to do so:

- **Don't give everything away.** More information isn't always better. It can lead to analysis paralysis. Stick to general information, and ask visitors to fill in a form to get a more detailed brochure, schedule a call or come to an event.
- **Keep the next action small**. It's tempting to ask for too much in an enquiry form. But the longer the form, the fewer the people who will fill it in. Stick to the bare essentials: name and email address, with phone number being optional and perhaps an optional field for the desired start date. As mentioned in Chapter 9, besides these visible fields, you can append hidden fields to capture more information without having to ask the prospective student for it.

13.5 CONCLUSION

Landing pages are a critical link in the online recruitment chain. To capture as many interested prospective students as possible, these pages should be mobile-friendly and focused, and should build trust and inspire action.

In this chapter I've discussed the final step in setting up your student recruitment search campaign. In the next chapter, I'll cover some of the special features of recruiting international students with search advertising.

14

Recruiting students internationally

Online advertising can be a great, cost-effective way to get more applications from abroad. To be successful, though, international online campaigns need to be different in a number of ways. That is, they need to

1. be **tailored** to the **target country**,
2. offer more opportunities for **online engagement**,
3. be written in **appropriate languages**, and
4. cover **different topics**.

14.1 TAILOR YOUR CAMPAIGN TO THE TARGET COUNTRY

While your programme is going to be essentially the same for all students, it will be perceived differently in different countries. The subject you offer may be hot in one market and less so in another. You'll be compared to different institutions. In some countries you may be considered a premium option, in others, an affordable alternative.

This means that if you're serious about recruiting students from a specific country, you need to treat your online recruitment effort there as a separate campaign. Be sure to do the legwork needed to understand how prospective students from that country perceive your course offerings.

14.2 OFFER OPPORTUNITIES FOR ONLINE ENGAGEMENT

If you're a UK-based institution trying to recruit in, say, Mexico, prospective students will not be able to show up for an open day to get a feel for your institution. Thus, it's even more important than usual to offer options for getting to know your institution. These can include the following:

- **Webinars**. The talks held during open days can also be offered in the form of webinars.
- **Videos**. Having videos of your institution, the students, the town and facilities makes a big difference. Prospective students will get a more realistic impression than when they have to rely on words and images alone.
- **Virtual campus tours**. These are similar to videos, but they allow for more self-directed exploration.
- **Communities**. Few sources of information are more effective than prospective students' own peers. Put prospective students in touch with student ambassadors on a forum of your own, or set up groups in country-relevant social networks: for example, Facebook, Vkontakte (Russia) or WeChat (China). You can also find ways to tap into your alumni network.
- **Local activities**. If you're going to organise an event or attend a student fair in the target country, be sure to advertise this

and mention it on the landing page. Serious prospects will probably come by and say "Hi!"

14.3 ADVERTISE IN THE APPROPRIATE LANGUAGES

In which language should you address prospective students? The standard response, especially in English-speaking countries is "In English, of course. They'll need to speak English to study here anyway."

However, if all your information is in English, and you're serious about recruiting in a non–English-speaking country, you'll bump into the following issues:

- **Missed out keywords**. You *could* show English ads in, say, Germany. But when people search with German keywords, your ads won't show. If you limit yourself to English keywords only, you'll be competing with the entire world for a limited number of clicks.
- **Excluded parents**. Parents are important stakeholders. In many cases, they foot the bill. And depending on the culture, they will have some say or even the final say in the choice of programme. While your prospective students may speak English, their parents might not.

In short, if you're aiming to recruit students in non–English-speaking countries, consider investing in ads and content in the local languages.

14.4 COVER TOPICS THAT MATTER TO INTERNATIONAL STUDENTS

When you promote your courses to domestic students, a lot of information is already known. For international students, be sure to cover the following:

- **What it's like to live in the city and at the university**. Studying is about more than formally acquiring knowledge and skills. Try to give a taste of what the total experience will be like.
- **How to choose the right programme**. If you can help prospective students choose the best-fitting programme at the outset – through an online assessment tool, for example – it will make your institution a more attractive choice. Moreover, you can prevent a lot of heartache down the road.
- **How others like them have experienced your institution**. Testimonials from a diverse group of both current students and alumni can paint a clear picture of the culture at your institution. Such testimonials can also help prospective students see the kinds of career your programme can prepare them for.
- **How to make it all happen**. Don't forget the nuts and bolts. It takes courage to decide to study abroad. But by breaking down how to find housing and funding, you help reduce the fear factor and make your institute and its staff more approachable.

14.5 CONCLUSION

Online campaigns can be a great and cost-effective tool for recruiting students from certain target countries. To make these campaigns successful, you can apply everything that has been covered in this book. In addition, think of each target country as needing a separate campaign with its own research, ad copy, content and follow-up, possibly in another language.

15

Working with agencies

Many universities choose to have agencies oversee their paid search campaigns. If you've made your way through the book up to here, you'll have a good understanding of what a digital marketing agency should do to help you in your recruitment efforts. All the same, there are a number of typical challenges in partnering with agencies. In this chapter I'll focus on the following:

- knowledge of the education sector,
- expectations,
- ad account ownership.

15.1 KNOWLEDGE OF THE EDUCATION SECTOR

Recruiting students is a very different ball game from selling concert tickets or driving e-commerce sales. When selecting an agency, ensure that they have experience in marketing educational institutions or, failing that, in campaigns that involve high-stakes personal decisions. Prospective students are deciding where to invest several years of their time and a considerable chunk of money. The type of marketing that is appropriate here requires a multi-step approach and is very different from selling lower-ticket items online.

A good agency understands that close collaboration with you and your team is essential for achieving success. A mediocre agency will focus only on their own KPIs: “But we got you lots of clicks and brochure downloads!” Don’t be shy to ask for related case studies, or specify this in your request for proposals (RFP).

15.2 EXPECTATIONS

A common pitfall when working with agencies is to leave all the planning to them. This kind of brief is very common: “We have a budget of €xxxxx to promote our faculty’s programmes. Could you give us a proposal for how to spend this?” Instead, meet with your staff and go through the planning exercise described in Chapter 10 (Putting it all together). Then share the outcome with prospective agencies. Ask them to comment and perhaps to challenge some of the underlying assumptions.

An agency that values partnership will jump at the chance to add value in this way. Agencies that are more transaction oriented may drop out of your selection process here. During the campaign evaluate the agency’s performance based on the planning exercise mentioned above. Make sure the agency sticks to your plan. If they begin to diverge from it in ways you don’t approve, intervene before it’s too late. In some cases, of course, it’s your original plan that will have to be altered.

15.3 AD ACCOUNT OWNERSHIP

I've seen schools commit large amounts of money to agencies and not have access to the accounts used to run the campaigns. There are two problems with this.

The first problem concerns **data ownership**. Statistics on which ads and keywords are most valuable belong to you, not to your agency. You've paid Google to show ads and the agency to manage the campaign. Should you decide to switch agencies, you'll want them to start where your previous agency left off. Moreover, on privacy grounds, it's much better if you ultimately control who accesses this data.

The second problem has to do with **transparency**. If you own the ad account used to run the campaigns, you can monitor performance on your own terms, dig into campaigns at will and bring in a third-party expert if needed. If your agency controls access to this data, they can pick a few stats that look good and send you a monthly report.

Fortunately, there is a simple way for you to own the data and to give agencies the level of access you think appropriate: the Google manager account.[8] Through this account, agencies can link to a customer's account. To request access, all that's needed is the customer's account number. In this way you can give the agency all the access it needs to run campaigns and even to pay on your behalf, if this is necessary. At the same time, you'll remain the ultimate account owner.

8 https://support.google.com/google-ads/answer/7459601

15.4 CONCLUSION

It's often external agencies that manage search campaigns for student recruitment. This can work well, provided the agency has sufficient understanding of and involvement in your strategy and planning. But your institution needs to maintain ultimate control over who accesses the ad account.

16

Conclusion

Student recruitment is a process. Too often, we get lost in the tactics. Tactics can be useful but only when they're connected to an overall strategy and monitored to ensure they are performing well. In this book, I've gone beyond how to execute the "tactics" of SEA and also included how it can be tightly linked to your overall recruitment strategy.

I hope that this book has given you an overview of what's possible with SEA, and how to go about achieving your goals. Managing SEA campaigns and everything around it is hard work, but when done well, the results can be quick and rewarding. I wish you success with your student recruitment campaigns.

If you have any questions or would like to know more, you'll find additional resources as well as a form to get in touch with me on my author website: guusgoorts.com.

ANNEXES

Resources

All professionals have a toolbox with essential tools. Here are the essential and recommended tools that I rely on as a digital education marketer.

ONLINE COURSES AND BOOKS

Google Skillshop (https://skillshop.withgoogle.com/)

Google Skillshop has an up-to-date collection of courses that teach the fundamentals of the complete set of Google tools. The focus is technical – don't expect to find much in the way of strategy. Still, it's the most important source for what's possible with Google's current tools.

P. Marshall, M. Rhodes and B. Todd, *Ultimate Guide to Google AdWords*, Irvine, California: Entrepreneur Media, Inc., 2017.

I consider this the Bible of Google Search. And I'm not alone. This book takes you from absolute beginner to pro by covering everything there is to know about squeezing the maximum out of your Google campaigns. Despite the depth it's a very approachable book with practical examples that inspire you to multiply the outcomes of your campaigns.

Guusgoorts.com

Digital marketing moves at such a speed that this book will be outdated the moment it rolls off the press. On my personal website I'll keep you up to date on the latest developments in digital marketing that are relevant for the education sector.

SOFTWARE

Landing pages: Unbounce, Leadpages, Instapage, Hubspot

You have to be able to tailor what prospective students see when they click your ad. This is often hard to achieve on the general website. The tools listed above allow you to quickly create, test and modify landing pages for your campaign. Hubspot does a lot more.

- Unbounce.com
- Leadpages.com
- Instapage.com
- Hubspot.com

CRM

There are countless CRMs, and which is best for your institution depends on so many factors that I can't really advise on it here. From a marketing point of view, it's important that the CRM is set up to capture source data ("Which campaign brought this lead to us in the first place?") and to keep track of all communications with the (prospective) student.

You may already be locked into a certain set-up. If not, Mailchimp is a very basic option for automated recruitment-related follow-up. It's a good CRM to get started with, even if you only use it temporarily.

- Mailchimp.com

Gaconnector

Gaconnector can extract source data (how someone found your website) from Google Analytics and make it show up in your CRM. It's only when you have the full picture that you can know whether your campaigns are actually working.

- Gaconnector.com

List of Figures

Printed in Great Britain
by Amazon